BONUS EDITION!
50 NEW pages of Cool Stuff!

By Katie Leigh
& Will Ryan

Other books by Will Ryan

The Plain an' Simple Get Well Book – Sunbeam Press

The Germ Book – Sunbeam Press

Animation Art (consulting editor) – Harper Design

The King's Beard – Random House

Who Are You, Sue Snoo? – Random House

Me & Duke – IconoClassics

The Tiny Little Book of Cowboy Haiku
– Oxnard University Press

The Biffle & Shooster Guide to Proper Etiquette
– Oxnard University Press

The Biffle & Shooster Comic Book Compendium – Fleagle

Other book by Katie Leigh

My Personal Diary, 2011—(unpublished)

Printed in U.S.A.
FIRST EDITION JULY 2015
SECOND PRINTING AUGUST 2015
NEW BONUS EDITION SEPTEMBER 2020
Cover Photo: (circa 1983) Tabi Cooper
Interior photos: (2015) Alysha Nicole
Bonus chapter photo: Vinny Jaey
Will's drawings: © MMXVII, MMXX Will Ryan

Oxnard University Press
"Where the Ink Hits the Page . . . Every Time."
Box 3551 * 1217 Wilshire Boulevard * Santa Monica, California 90408

Dedication

To all our faithful listeners
of, lo, these many years!
W.R.

And to everybody else too!
K.L.

CONTENTS

Foreword by Phil Lollar

FOREWORD

By Phil Lollar

I've been asked by Will Ryan and Katie Leigh to write a foreword for this book. Or perhaps I should say that I've been asked by "Katie Leigh and Will Ryan" to write a foreword for this book.

You see, the two of them have decided to share equal billing on this work. Half the time one person's name will be listed first. And the other half of the time, the other person's name Will be listed first. That's fine with me, but I understand that this decision is currently wreaking havoc at the publisher's office. And I have an eerie feeling that this bizarre crediting procedure will no doubt create similar confusion in the marketplace.

I'm not sure which of the two authors came up with the idea of alternate billing, but I'm kinda thinking it was Katie. I could be wrong. I've been wrong before. Katie will tell you.

Come to think of it, it's a good thing that one of Will's interview questions for Katie wasn't "Can you name some of the times when Phil Lollar was wrong?" because she could rattle off a long list of situations wherein I was actually right but she thought I was wrong. She probably has enough of them to fill a good chapter or two. And if that were to happen, this book would be too way long and then there probably wouldn't be any space for this Foreword.

Which would be perfectly fine with me, because I've got better things to do with my time than write a Foreword for two people who can't even decide whose name should be listed first. Among other things, I have to finish another "***ADVENTURES IN ODYSSEY***" script today, and it's a good one too! It's about Connie and Eugene, or possibly "Eugene and Connie" deciding to write a book together. They finish the book, but then . . . they can't decide on whose name should come first in the credits! Needless to say, hilarity ensues.

I don't know where I come up with all these ideas.

Enjoy the book.

PHIL LOLLAR is the co-creator of the popular radio series "*ADVENTURES IN ODYSSEY*," which is heard throughout the world and on over 2,400 radio stations in North America. He is also the co-creator of "Jungle Jam and Friends," "Little Dogs on the Prairie," "Iliad House," and several other shows, and is a Communication Studies and Cinema Studies professor at Azusa Pacific University in Azusa, California. Phil is the co-founder, with Katie Leigh and Will Ryan, of Fort Blanket Revue, a nascent multimedia threat to gloom. This is his first Foreword. Even if Katie Leigh claims otherwise.

1

Ave!

In which we meet our *dramatis personae*
and literary plans are devised

Katie

Who starts?

WILL

You do.

Katie

Why me? Why not you?

WILL

You already started.

Katie

Oh.

WILL

Pray continue.

Katie

Okay. Hi everybody! I'm Katie Leigh and I play Connie Kendall on "***ADVENTURES IN ODYSSEY***."

WILL

Which is . . .

Katie

Which is, if you don't already know (which I doubt because, if you didn't, then you probably wouldn't be reading this in the first place) the famous audio series heard throughout the world and on over two thousand radio stations in North America.

How was that?

WILL
Very good. Now my turn?

Katie
All yours!

WILL
Greetings and salutations, fellow Earthings! I'm Will Ryan and I play Eugene Meltsner, the be-goggled sesquipedalian, in that self-same series.

KATIE
And what about Harlow Doyle?

WILL
Indeed, I perform his voice too. And those of others, as well.

Katie
And what's a "sasqui-per . . . "?

WILL

A "sesquipedalian" is a person habituated to the employment of verbiage of notable heft.

Katie

You mean: A person who uses a lotta big words?

WILL

Indubitably!

Katie

And what is the name of that show, again?

WILL

"*ADVENTURES IN ODYSSEY*," the wireless series which celebrated its 30th anniversary beginning in the year of 2017.

Katie

Wait! You said "celebrated"?

WILL

So I did.

Katie

Why the past tense? This book comes out before that.

WILL
Statistically speaking, more people will be reading this book after the year 2017 than prior or during it.

Katie
Really? They've got statistics on the future already?

WILL
Well, more precisely, they're statistical probabilities predicated upon existing data subjected to learned extrapolation.

Katie
Well, you've convinced me.

WILL
Of what?

Katie
That you're the voice of Eugene!

WILL
Oh. I see what you mean. Hmmm.

Katie
Are you humming or thinking?

WILL

The latter. Since you brought up the sore subject of audience misidentification . . . I should mention that the principal reason I have agreed to collaborate with you on this tome is that I perceive it as an opportunity to shatter a certain long-standing shibboleth.

Katie

Well, that's nice, you—What?!

WILL

I intend to correct a commonly-held, long-standing misapprehension on the part of the listenership of "***Adventures in Odyssey***."

Katie

Oh. You wanna straighten something out.

WILL
Indeed.

Katie

You think some people have the wrong idea about something.

WILL
Precisely.

Katie

And you wanna use this book to show those people they were wrong.

WILL

Indubitably.

Katie

So . . . what's the deal?

WILL

By "what's the deal?" is it your intention to inquire "What, pray tell, is the misapprehension under which many of our listeners are laboring?"

Katie

Um . . . Yeah.

WILL

For some reason, people are under the impression that we, i.e., Katie and Will, are similar in personality to the characters we play, i.e. Connie and Eugene!

Katie

We're not?

WILL

Of course we're not. You dare take umbrage at this contention?

Will the real EUGENE MELTSNER PLEASE stand up!

A

B

C

D

E

F

Can you guess the identities of these Meltsner look-alikes?

(Answers on last page)

• 20 •

Katie

How do I know? I have no idea what you just said!

WILL

Well, we can get into all that later. Let's use this space to discuss the rest of this book.

Katie

Okay! Here's the scoop, everybody: Will and I decided to add to the 30th Anniversary festivities by writing a book about our adventures in radio. And in cartoons. And in real-life. And in other places too!

WILL

"Other places"?

Katie

Sure. Other places!

WILL

Other places than real-life? Such as . . . ?

Katie

Well, like that time you dreamed I was a giant chicken and I was buying you an upside-down pizza pie for Lincoln's birthday.

WILL

Oh.

Katie
See?

WILL
Do we really have to mention that dream?

Katie
Not if you don't want me to.

WILL
I'd rather we didn't.

Katie
Okay. We won't.

WILL
Thank you.

Katie
You're welcome.

WILL
I mean, it's not the kind of thing I'd like to see plastered all over the place.

Katie
I understand.

WILL
I mean, it's not worth mentioning.

Katie
Agreed.

WILL
Or even alluded to.

Katie
Right.

WILL
And it's certainly not worth dwelling on.

Katie
I would never dwell on that dream where I was a giant chicken and I was buying you an upside-down pizza pie for Lincoln's birthday.

WILL
Ya know something?

Katie
What?

WILL
Neither would I!

Katie
Now that we've settled that, I have a question about the rest of the book.

WILL
The rest of the book?

Katie
You know the part that's not about the dream where I was a giant chicken.

WILL
. . . who was buying me an upside-down pizza pie?

Katie
. . . for Lincoln's birthday.

WILL
You mean there's more to this book than that? Good value!

Katie
I agree. But my question is: How exactly are you and I going to

An oblivious sesquipedalian, as observed by Prof. Zeus

write a whole book together? I mean, won't it be hard to combine two completely different writing styles?

WILL
Nope.

Katie
Why not?

WILL
Here's why not: We'll do the whole book in dialogue form!

Katie
I'm not sure . . .

WILL
What do you mean you're not sure? It's perfect!

Katie
Well, I'm not sure exactly what you mean by "in dialogue form"?

WILL
You know! Instead of page after page of paragraphs of narrative written in the First Person, everything in our book **WILL** be written like dialogue in a script.

Katie
Sounds weird.

WILL

Katie, it's the way we talk on the radio!

Katie

We do?

WILL

Yes, really! We'll do the book in dialogue, just the way we do dialogue on the radio show!

Katie

Oh, I get it! We'll ad-lib and argue with the writers about the grammar and logic!

WILL

I hope not. For one thing, this time *we* are the writers!

Katie

Yeah, that's sort of self-defeating, isn't it? Then what do you mean?

WILL

I mean the book will be presented as a transcribed discussion between the two of us. The way we talk to each other in Real Life.

Katie

Can people do that in a book?

WILL
Why not?

Katie
Well, won't it look funny on the page?

WILL
Huh?

Katie
I mean, isn't it kind of like cheating?

WILL
What do you mean?

Katie
Well, don't book readers expect and maybe even deserve a more thought-out, a more composed, a more—I don't know—a more "literary" experience?

WILL
What?

Katie
I mean, who ever heard of anybody reading an entire book filled up with nothing but a bunch of dialogue? Who would ever write such a ridiculous thing?

WILL
Um, Shakespeare?

Katie

Oh. Good point.

WILL

George Bernard Shaw?

Katie

Okay. I get it.

WILL

Noel Coward? Neil Simon? Paddy Chayesvsky? Arthur Miller?
Henrik Ibsen? Oscar Wilde? Jerome Lawrence and Robert E. Lee?
Sophocles? Euripides? Eumendides? Eupayferdes?

Katie

Alright! Alright already!

WILL

So waddaya think?

Katie

I'm not sure. I mean, do the lines of dialogue have to be really
short, the way they usually are in a script or could we ramble on a
lot longer, kind of giving little essays or soliloquies or something
without all that snappy back and forth kind of patter that makes a
scene punchy and rhythmic and sort of realistic-sounding, but is
maybe kinda disconnected or whatever?

WILL

Huh? Sorry. You were rattling on so much I started thinking about
lunch.

Katie

Well, I guess that does it.

WILL

Does what?

Katie

Answers my question.

WILL

Not necessarily.

Katie

Oh?

WILL

For example, I would be speaking through my metaphorical hat were I to deny the simple fact that it would not be outside the purview of our proposed stylistic approach to take advantage of a certain technique employed by such figures as the immortal Boz—that most Dickensian of all writers—in using an authorial voice whilst discussing, say, the epoch of incredulity and the season of Light in his notable lead-in to "A Tale of Two Cities," or the revered Carroll (the Reverend Dodgson, if you **WILL**) in describing Alice's interior monologue upon being presented with a two-word directive from—of all things—a bottle containing an indeterminate substance, as well as by countless other scriveners of merit, for in sooth such esteemed literary practitioners have clearly demonstrated the efficacy—not to say the elegance, the effulgence, the insouciance—of skillful employment of the so-called run-on sentence.

Agree?

Katie

Huh? Sorry. You were rattling on so much I started thinking about lunch.

WILL

Hmm.

Katie

But if you were saying we could rattle on without interruption in our Question and Answer chapters, I'm all for it.

WILL

Good. Agreed. So . . . what say? Time for Chapter Two?

Katie

Chapter Two? Does that mean we just wrote Chapter One?

WILL

Yup.

Katie

YEA! LUNCH!

CHAPTER

2

The Will Ryan Interview
Conducted by Katie Leigh

In which Katie, astonishingly, revises well-laid plans

Katie

Okay. I changed my mind since the Introduction.

WILL

Huh?

Katie

Yeah. Now I wanna do the book like this: In this chapter, I ask a question and then you answer it—for as little or as long as you like.

WILL

No interruptions from you?

Katie

No interruptions from me.

WILL

Really.

Katie

Really!

WILL

Hmmm.

Katie

And then I ask the next question and so on. See? And then in the next chapter we switch places—and you don't interrupt me! Cool, huh? So, Will, are you ready for my first question?

WILL
You mean the one you just posed and to which I am currently responding?

Katie
No. That one doesn't count.

WILL
Oh. I couldn't tell.

Katie
Well, now you know. So . . . for my first "official" question: What do you think of this Q and A format I came up with for these interview chapters of the book?

WILL
Well, first of all, I was hoping this Q and A section might be Multiple Choice, but so far I guess it's not.

But apart from that . . . I think it's a great format because, now that we're not employing the Dialogue approach, I can answer you without being interrupted all the time. See? No interruption by you! Finally, this tome can take on an intelligent flow of thought! Behold! You didn't interrupt me there either! And if were to I point out here that you have, on occasion, been known to display the fascinating ability of speaking faster than you can actually think, you won't be able to interrupt me again.

You see, in the previous sentence I might have expected you to intervene and point out that I had split an infinitive, but—*mirable dictu*—no such protestation occurred!

I must confess, however, to a slight feeling of dread regarding whatever answers may be found in the *next* chapter—the one wherein *you* provide the answers. So perhaps we should try to keep our answers short. Or, as I might have phrased it a moment earlier, it may be efficacious to limit the occurrences of sesquipedalianism and blathering in our interrogatory responses.

But, at least as far as this chapter is concerned, I commend you for your enlightened decision of allowing me a forum free of pesky intrusion!

Katie

Thank you. I think. Okay—on to my carefully thought-out list of questions! And remember—you have to treat each question seriously. First of all: What is your favorite donut?

WILL

The one I didn't eat, because that was the best thing for me to do.

I've probably eaten a total of four doughnuts (or donuts, as they've come to spelled) in the last three decades or so. Doughnuts used to be found at the "crafts table" on film sets, which might be where I last had a part of one.

When I was a kid, there was a doughnut shop across from our church, and as an occasional treat, Dad would buy doughnuts for each of the whole family afterwards. Most of us liked glazed doughnuts then, which were about as tricky as those doughnuts got. Oh yeah, and the jelly-filled ones too, which I think were a little more expensive.

Keep in mind that this was a rare treat. We only had ice cream, cake and soda pop on certain birthdays.

That's the way it was. Things seem to have changed in much of the United States since then.

About twenty years ago or so, a new well-financed doughnut chain popped up into the national consciousness. It bombarded America with public relations and marketing hokum. For a while, the mystique they had created caused long lines at their shops. Somebody gave me one of those doughnuts once, or at least a part of one. I couldn't taste the public relations hype, I could only taste the doughnut.

But those doughnuts we had as kids were, in fact, really special!

Katie
Have you ever fixed anything in an interesting way?

WILL
Hey, are you talking about election-rigging? I hope not, because

election fraud has become a plague of the land and I abhor the practice. It is an abomination unto the republic!

If, however, you're referring to handyman type stuff, I'd like to brag a little about all the many triumphs, major and minor, which I've managed to pull off in this area, but I wouldn't know where to start!

And that's for this one simple reason: Try as I might, I can't actually think of a one.

I do recall one time quite a few years ago, when I accomplished something of an ergonomic nature. A band I was in was having a meeting with Bob Kimple, the great businessman, manager and promoter who changed the life of me and of many others. We were all standing around in a room talking for quite a while. I was getting tired of standing. But then . . . I noticed a simple wooden chair in another part of the room and, after a bit of thinking, a practical idea having to do with physical reality actually formed within my mind!

I don't like to brag, but here's what I did: I walked over to that chair and brought it back to where I'd been standing for ten minutes and sat down in it. Bob laughed out loud because he had seen my thought process as it unfolded: me seeing the chair, me thinking how nice it would be to sit down, the imaginary light-bulb going on in my head, me bringing the chair over to my spot, me sitting on the chair, and evidently some smile of satisfaction for my Neanderthal accomplishment. It was a kind of revelation: to realize that such things could be done. I have tried to apply this kind of thought-into-action dynamic ever since.

If you just read that little story, you're probably wondering if I'm kidding. I'm not. This event took place over thirty years ago in Lakewood, Ohio and it still looms large in my memory.

Ya know, there used to be Fix-It shops all over this country, but the very idea seems anachronistic in these days of throw-away items. Maybe Harlow Doyle should open one.

Katie
Are you the oldest in your family?

WILL
So far, but several cousins are catching up.

It wasn't always thus. When I started out, *both* of my parents had a head start. In fact, *all* of my relatives used to be older than I was! NOW look what's happened!

Katie
Is there anyone on Odyssey you relate to more than Eugene?

WILL
Sure. That talking chicken in Twi-Life Zone episode! We're very much alike.

Will the real EUGENE MELTSNER PLEASE stand up!

G

H

I

J

K

L

Can you guess the identities of these Meltsner look-alikes?

(Answers on last page)

I also relate to the character Jimmy Barclay, voiced by David Griffin. I always feel so much sympathy for Jimmy and his predicaments. And a large part of that is Dave's voice. And we've all seen ("heard," actually) Jimmy grow up before our very . . . um, ears. And that familiarity adds another layer of empathy.

Connie Kendall is another really sympathetic character, but I always get her mixed up with the actress who plays her, so I'm not unbiased. Of course, I can't boast of actually understanding either of them!

And speaking of incomprehension . . .

Harlow Doyle, private eye, is similar to me in that: were I to suddenly become a private eye, I too would undoubtedly find myself outside of my area of competence. Naturally, I would hope that experience and study would allow me to better myself in that vocation, but – who knows?

Katie
Do you speak any other languages?

WILL
Yes, but I usually don't know what I'm saying in them.

My old friend and hero Paul Winchell, on the other hand, spoke six languages rather fluently. I witnessed his skill with my own eyes at the International Ventriloquist's Association annual convention in Las Vegas in the 1990s, as he chatted away happily for hours with people from all over the world. He had a brilliant mind.

Katie
Where did you grow up?

WILL
In and around my hometown.

Katie
What was it like?

WILL
Fortunately, it happened so gradually that the only clue I had that anything of an altitudinous nature was occurring was that I seemed to need new clothes every year or so. Fortunately, I was not alone in this regard. Most of my contemporaries were growing at a similar rate, ergo few of us were really aware of the fate in store for us: to ultimately become similar in some respects to those towering creatures known as "grown ups" who all seemed to, for some unknown reason, share a completely different perspective on the world around them.

Katie
How did you get your own radio show and TV shows in Cleveland?

WILL

I'll never forget the name of the guy who gave me my start in radio, although it slips my mind at the moment. Just kidding. Actually, my good pal Bob Kimple gave me my behind-the-scenes start in radio. And a few years later legendary radio performer Bill Randle gave me "the big push" into on-air radio. You can see earlier documentary footage of Bill give a relatively-unknown lad named Elvis Presley "the big push" in a movie called "This Is Elvis." Bill was one of the smartest humans I've ever known.

Katie
Chocolate or Vanilla?

WILL

I suppose I could say swirl or possibly strawberry, but this is evidently an important subject and I should treat it appropriately.

In my early days, chocolate was much more exotic and absolutely the universal preference. Only wacky, free-thinking, incomprehensible weirdos seemed to favour vanilla! The chocolate then available to us also had more flavour than the relatively bland vanilla of the brands we were subject to in those days.

Nowadays, some high-end vanilla products can have a great, strong vanilla taste! And the same goes for chocolate: the variety of available chocolate flavours seems to have improved.

So I say: to each his own.

Katie

What kind of weather do you like?

WILL

I don't mind London-type weather (also known as Manhattan-type weather, Cleveland-type weather, Detroit-type weather, Pittsburgh-type weather, Zelienople-type weather, etc.) in terms of the amount of annual sunshine.

I suppose Jamaica has the best climate.

I don't believe there's anyplace on this planet devoid of the possibility of typhoons, floods, draught, irritating amounts of snow and hail. Toss in things like earthquakes, fire, etc. and you've got the makings of all kinds of insurance scams and a good argument for space exploration.

Katie

How did you know you wanted to be an actor?

WILL

The check cleared.

Katie

Can you name all fifty states?

WILL

I'll try, employing cantorial compositions as mnemonics:

Characters who have yet to make it on to the show (*According to Will Ryan, anyway*). *From top left: Schmoidley Crump, critic; kindly Mrs. Malcolm, housewife and millionaire record collector; (center) Big Bob of "Little Bob's Veggie Burgers and Tacos"; Thurwood Findle, history professor and scholar; Patty Ryan, author's sister; Osgood Nogood, retired petty thief.*

Alabamy bound, Arkansas traveler, by the time I get to Arizona put on your rainbow shoes, the next time I see her Alaska . . .

Nothing with B? I guess there's Baja and Alta California. I live in the second one, but the other one's below the arbitrary border.

And speaking of nada, nothing could be finer than to be in Carolina: North and South, California here I am. Colorado rocky mountain: Hi!

In the words of Perry Como, what did Delaware?

Nothing with E? How about Euterpia? Eek? Elvisonia?

The land of the monkey-doodle-doo: Florida! But how about that other ever-popular Marxist state: Fredonia?

Georgia on my mind,

They're wearin' 'em higher in Hawaii. (I'm saving the "New"s for the letter N.) How about Hokumland?

Away back home in Indiana (an oft-performed song of the original Hollywood Cartoon Band), let's sing a little song and make a joyful Illinois, where the S is "ilent."

Nothing with J? How about Jackalopia?

I might take a boat or a plane to the state of Kansas, and write a song about the blue, blue grass of Kentucky.

Louisiana, I declare – if I'm quoting Bing correctly.

Uh oh, now we come to the Ms and Ns. Lots of states here!

Oh how I wish again I was in Michigan, ol' Massachusetts in de cold, cold ground, so let's remember the Maine, and as the afore-mentioned Perry Como might have well inquired: where did Maryland? Mister Ippi's wife might know.

She wore a brand New Jersey in old New York and nueva New

Mexico. Many songs have been written about New Hampshire, but few have been sung.

As they say in Japan: Ohio. Where have all the Oregon? (Actually, a native would fire off a 44 Oregon.)

I suppose people still have a mania for doing the Pennsylvania Polka.

Ideas for Q states: Quackland, Quiveria, Quetzalcoatl (new name for New Mexico?).

Rhode Island, a state so big it takes two words to say it! And no other state dares annoy it by also beginning with an R. How about: the ever-popular Ruritania? Or Rubbleonia?

No states with S other than Bajas Carolina and Dakota? A great one might be Seymour! Or Shambola? Slickaroo? Scrumbleton? Sphygmomanomita – the state of happy health!

"And twenty-three times the size of Tennessee" to quote a song I've been singing this week. What a great native-American name for a state! And Ellwood W. Dellwood loves spelling it! The song I've been singing, by the way, is called "Twice the Size of Texas."

No U states other than Utah? Uglyland? Urbania? The ever-popular Utopia! How about Upper Lowdownia? Last I checked, there were over 10,000 Utes in areas the white man decided to call Utah and Colorado – and we never hear a word about them.

They carried him back to ol' Virginia.

But from West Virginny they came to stay. . . with Washington, who wondered: Wyoming?

I suppose a state named Xenophonia would not hold appeal to potential immigrants. Not sure about Yudnik or Zinky.

I'm not sure if I named all fifty, but I hope I get credit for some of the new state names I came up with!

In fact, here are 26 more, which I've listed BELOW in a secret system of organization, which may be recognized by the abecedarians in our midst.

Hey! Maybe we can use these names on the moon!

WILL'S NAMES FOR NEW LUNAR STATES
(Or possibly for elves)

Abadaba-dibaduba

Balonia

Cavitanium

Dunderkopfvelt

Effulgia

Fwippy

Garglonium

Hoolipooliland

Iggledip

Jubblekee

Lalalalala

Monkeyshinoleum

New Noonoo

Oopsland

Piggleplex

Queezee

Razzle Frazzle

Sud Iggledip

Therbil

Ultimato

Vapidia

West Iggledip

Xeepy Island

Yeefledum

Ziggleplop

Æpullvania

Katie

What do you like to do for fun?

WILL

Everything. But it isn't always appropriate.

Katie

If you could pick your own name, what would it be?

WILL

Probably not Smiggly G. Heimlich-Vachupo. Wouldn't fit on a marquee.
And it might make people say "Gesundheit."

How about Charlie? Everybody likes people named Charlie. Reminds you of Charlie Chaplin, Charlie Chase, Champagne Charlie, Good Time Charlie, Bonnie Prince Charlie, Charlie Chan, Charlie Woodrum, Charlie McNaughton—all fun people!

I'm not certain that's the moniker for me, though.

Basil Rathbone has already been taken. Great name. Likewise Elvis Presley, Fess Parker, Minnie Minoso, Mickey Mantle, Walt Disney, Spike Jones, Stan Freberg and other names which, in my less-altitudinous days, always seemed to me to have some magic attached to them. Another such example: Rocky Colavito.

Actually, about ten years ago I happened to be chatting with my friend, the famous actress Anne Jeffries at the corner of

(Mister Whittaker, or possibly Bentley Barlock, as envisioned by Will Ryan)

Bentley and Barlock and I, struck by the euphony of our environ, decided that—henceforth—my new name as a "serious" actor would be: Bentley Barlock! And thus was born: Bentley Barlock! Known to the world as . . . Bentley Barlock, the greatest Shakesperean actor of his—or any other—generation and known to his intimates as: Mister Bentley Barlock!

But leave us not forget the favours bestowed annually by Her Majesty, for in some not too distant future, we may well find ourselves leaping to our feet and shouting for yet another curtain call from: Sir Bentley Barlock!

But, back to the question, the name"Will Ryan," although perhaps not as dazzling as "Basil Rathbone," is arguably not without a certain amount of magic and does indeed fit on a marquee rather neatly!

Katie

Do you like Eugene being married?

WILL

I thought that, dramatically, it would not be a good idea.
In fiction, and sometimes in life, marriage can also diminish a
character's audience appeal. Here's a really bad example: Imagine how popular the Beatles might have become if, when they
started out, one of their members—the one with the long hair,
as I seem to recall—hadn't already tied the knot. Why, instead
of being merely the world-wide phenomenon they became,
they could have "really" been big!

But I will say that by now I've got used to the fact that Katrina
appears in an episode every once in a while.

Of course Audrey Waselewski, the modern voice of Katrina, is
a terrific actress and a wonderful person. We are lucky to have
her on the show. I'm very lucky to be able to work with her.
She should be heard more frequently on the series, but perhaps
in other, even more vital and thankful, roles—playing characters who are more frequent in appearance!

After some recent episodes with Audrey, I realized there could
be a Rob and Laura Petrie dynamic to their scenes, which
could be fun. But I still don't think the target audience of AIO
finds domesticity particularly thrilling. I mean, look at all the
characters on the series who've turned out, after a few episodes

or a few years of episodes, to be undercover spies! This "Mitch" character, whom I've only encountered in the series but once, is suddenly a spy – and so is his wife! And after several years as a regular character on the series, Jason Whittaker was revealed to be an international spy! And then, incredibly, so was Whit! And so was Lucy Cunningham-Schultz! (No wait. That last one hasn't happened. Yet. Should I put a "spoiler alert" here?)

It's some kind of a weird epidemic, like the episode wherein everybody (Paul, Walker, Katie, the dog, et al.) turns out to be high-school class valedictorian!

So maybe, just to keep things interesting, Eugene and Katrina should follow in the footsteps of Joe Wilson and Valerie Plame-Wilson and become international spies who are married to each other. And should such an event occur, let us all hope no heartless administration official will once again put their entire operation in jeopardy by spilling the beans!

On the other hand, the last I ever heard, Eugene was nineteen years old. That's way too soon for him to settle down. Although he is in many ways a genius, he's also clearly not ready to drive a car or tie his shoes, let alone sign a mortgage or tie the knot.

Katie
If Eugene had his own show, what would he do on it?

WILL
On his first series he would give great lectures on esoteric,

Will the real CONNIE KENDALL PLEASE stand up!

A

B

C

D

E

F

Can you guess the identities of these Connie Kendall look-alikes?
(Answers on last page)

interesting subjects – possibly punctuating them with pleasingly plangent performances upon the ukulele. Naturally, he would be assisted by Constance Kendall, his "vox populi" sidekick.

Next season, as that show continues in production, his all-new series would be a mystery series, wherein the solutions of the puzzles are dependent upon obscure knowledge. Naturally, he would be assisted by Constance Kendall, his "vox populi" amanuensis.

His third show would be a crossword or sudoku puzzle challenge between himself and his guests. This show would require very little of his time (five episodes could be shot in a morning), so that he may continue working simultaneously on the first two series. Naturally, he would be assisted by Constance Kendall, his "vox populi" acolyte and letter-turner.

Since the only people who seem to be rewarded these kinds of "failing upward" show biz careers are usually William Morris Agency clients—or maybe CAA—Eugene would doubtless be forced have to have stultifying show biz people like Whoopie Goldbrick and Kevin Waterworld as guests on his shows; fellow clients whose negotiated presence which would so annoy his sensibilities that he'd quit in disgust. Then, in an attempt to placate him and incidentally make even more unearned money for all concerned, the agency would make him Executive Producer on a bunch of television shows with which he had absolutely nothing to do.

Katie

Wow! You've given that a lot of thought! Now I repeat: What do you like to do for fun?

WILL

I guess my earlier answer sounded flip. It was meant to be humourous, but it's also accurate.

Because seriously: many of the smartest people I know or have met seem to be able to have as much fun as possible wherever they are, whatever they're doing.

But if the question refers to pre-planned, organized, scheduled fun, here's what's on my current calendar:

This morning I'm working on this book, responding to all your snoopy inquiries. And guess what? It's fun!

At noon today there I'll be at a lunch meeting of the Hotcha Club, an informal society of nebulous size (about six core members) who are all show biz professionals. We're celebrating the birthday of one of our own, Miriam Nelson. Miriam's a really active person who drives all over southern California choreographing shows, directing productions, helping run a non-profit charity she co-founded several decades ago which raises about a million dollars a year for worthy children's causes and doing all kinds of other positive things. Miriam starred in her own one-woman show last year, playing to standing-room-only crowds, in which she told amazing but true stories about her life and

Connie Kendall borrowing Harlow Doyle's "sell" phone
(He's been trying to sell it for years!)

career, spiced up with a some singing and dancing. She also saw her first autobiography published this past year, a very well-written account of her life on Broadway and in films, cabaret, television, Disneyland and other interesting places. She choreographed the Oscars a couple of times, the opening day of a place called Disneyland, the opening ceremonies of the Autry Museum, many films and dozens of night club acts for some of the biggest names in show business. And, to my wondering eyes, she directed her very first "music video" (or "Soundie" if you prefer, or my own neologism: "CineSong"). It's the song "Rhythm Rides the Range," performed by Will Ryan & the Cactus County Cowboys and she did a swell job!

Oh, did I mention that Miriam turned 95 recently? She's figured out one or two things in her time and I guarantee you she does as much as she can "for fun!"

And speaking of fun, I think it would be fun to turn the metaphorical tables and interview you, Katie Leigh, in the next chapter!

CHAPTER

3

The Katie Leigh Interview
Conducted by Will Ryan

In which metaphorical tables are, indeed, turned

WILL

Which is your favorite AIO episode?

Katie

I have two . . . "License to Drive" and "Back to Bethlehem." Both of them star me and you!

WILL

Which is your least favorite AIO episode?

Katie

My least was one about witnessing with some guy Connie was dating.

WILL

You've been playing Connie Kendall on AIO for thirty years now, so can you tell us something we don't know about her, like how tall she is or her middle name?

Katie

Yes. She is my height and she forgot her middle name.

WILL

Do you ever make mistakes when you record AIO episodes?

Katie

You mean say the wrong thing? Yes, but rarely. Just kidding. Luckily, we're recording and not "live" so we can re-do things. I don't mind making mistakes, but I really love it when you do. It makes me laugh and laugh and laugh!

WILL

What are some of your favorite characters you've done the voices for?

Katie

Of course Baby Rowlf on "The Muppet Babies" was my absolute favorite for so many reasons. I was always a huge Muppets fan, so getting to be one is still beyond belief! The characters that no one thinks are me are the best. I voiced Han Solo-as-a-boy for a Cartoon Network Lego "Star Wars" special. I also dubbed the voice of the maharajah in "Indiana Jones and the Temple of Doom." Did you know that?

WILL

I remember! What was it like working with Jim Henson?

Katie

You should know! As for me, it was unbelievable and nerve-wracking! On our first day of recording, he was there. The character I played was a character he created and voiced. I was so afraid of imitating Jim in front of him and doing a bad job. So every time Rowlf had a line, I would ask him to read it first.

WILL

Have you ever done voice work in another language?

Katie

Si! I have done a lot of post-production for TV and movies and now internet and radio in Spanish. I also have gotten to use some French and German while working on movies.

WILL

Who's your agent?

Katie

Same as yours: Arlene Thornton of Arlene Thornton & Associates in Studio City, California.

WILL

Ah yes. The Greatest Talent Agent in the World! Changing the subject entirely, who are some of the weirdest people you've ever worked with?

Katie

Besides you? Bob Ridgely, Robert Easton. They all have "Bob" for a first name, I think. Bob Ridgely was really insane and would say outrageous things. Bob Easton was eccentric and I couldn't take my eyes off of him. But to me the really "weirdest" people are the unfriendly ones, because I can't understand that.

WILL

Who are some of the weirdest people you've never worked with?

Katie

Howard Hughes. Charlie Sheen.

WILL

Ten questions down. What's the dumbest recording session you ever did?

Katie

Well, once a friend of mine and I auditioned for a commercial together. We both got cast. When we showed up at the studio, they told us they wanted us to do it *exactly* like the audition. But when we asked them if they had the recording for us to hear what we had done a couple of weeks prior, they didn't have it. We just looked at each other like "you've got to be kidding! How are we going to remember exactly what we did?"

Another time I was in labor with my daughter at a recording session for six radio commercials. I got through three of them before I had to go home and give birth.

Then one time I got hired for a cereal commercial that featured the Gummi Bears. I got to the studio and discovered that my only line was "No." That was dumb . . . but fortuitous!

WILL

Who would you like to play you in the major motion picture "The Katie Leigh Story"?

(Connie Kendall—or is it her kid sister Jules?—
as envisioned by Will Ryan)

Katie

Good question. Well, if I didn't do it myself, then I think Meg Tilly should do it. And then maybe I could be her in "The Meg Tilly Story." Tee hee. On the other hand, as you've pointed out, Tracey Lyn Holland can play all of us!

WILL

I agree! She's great! If you didn't work as an actress, what kind of work would you do?

Katie

Well, I like teaching school (which I actually do now anyway, so I'm not sure that is a fair question). But my dream is to manage a spiritual retreat center and meet new people every week – kind of like the Timothy Center in Odyssey. In the mountains. By water. I just want to greet people and make sure everything's okay, kind of like a retreat hostess. But I don't wanna have to wear a uniform. Is there such a job as that?

WILL

When I see one, I'll let you know. Now – If you actually lived in the town of Odyssey, what kind of work would you do?

Katie

That's funny because I actually stumbled upon a real place that is just like the town of Odyssey. It's Winona Lake, Indiana. I don't know the zip code. I went there to work for the Masterworks Festival as an acting master (can you believe it?) and, seriously, the town is just like Odyssey! The ice cream shop there, Kelainey's, looks like Whit's End. So, maybe I would work at that ice cream shop. Or maybe I would be a voice actress working from home. Your questions are harder than mine.

WILL

Which is you favorite planet?

Katie

"LOL! Uranus, of course! No, just kidding. My favorite planet is Planet Hollywood.

WILL

Do you have any favorite movies?

Katie

I never get tired of watching "The Parent Trap" with Dennis Quaid and Lindsay Lohan. I think she should have won an Academy Award. I also really loved an old movie called "City of Angels," directed by Wim Wenders. But some of my favorite movies I saw with you. Remember in the old days when they would let us into the movie theaters for free right before the Academy Awards and Screen Actors Guild awards so we could see the movies and vote on them? You and I went to a lot of movies together and you will always be my best movie buddy. There are also lots of movies we didn't see together.

WILL

Are you now, or have you ever been a member of a masquerade party?

Katie

NOOOOOOOOOO! I really hate dressing up and that is why I am a voice actor and not a face actor. I barely remember to brush my hair. Well, I guess brushing my hair has nothing to do with masks, does it?

WILL

Can you discuss an interesting vacation you've had?

Katie

Several. I had a great one when I went to New York and saw my sister. She was getting an award. At that time, you were there working for Henson, writing "The Wubbulous World of Dr. Seuss." We had so much fun walking around New York city, and you took me to see the creature shop and your office. Then we bumped into Phil Proctor on the street and had brunch with him the next morning. Remember that? We also went to the top of the Empire State Building together . . . I think. Was that you?

And the before that, many years earlier, I had a great vacation in London where I stayed with Eric and Susan Goldberg, where I stayed in the same bed you had just stayed in while you were visiting Eric and Susan. On that trip I actually visited Jim Henson on the set of Labyrinth and he took me out to dinner with his daughter Cheryl. Isn't that funny how my two best vacations involve Jim Henson and you?

Finally in answer to this question, I took a road trip from Pennsylvania to Washington, D.C. with my kids. Then when I got home, the next Odyssey show we recorded was about a road trip from Pennsylvania to Washington, D.C. I relived every mile!

I've actually been to many places around the world, doing different things from backpacking throughout Europe to going on cruises in the Caribbean. I've never been to the Eastern seaboard.

Oh! I loved seeing how the canals worked when I was in Oregon City, Oregon. What about you?

WILL

After fifteen years on the Erie Canal, I've seen enough of those! Back on track, if you had to do one episode of "*ADVENTURES IN ODYSSEY*" over, which one would it be?

Katie

Dang! I'd have to listen to them again. But probably some with Mitch. That's because I think I had an attitude at the time that kept popping through the performances. I have heard many episodes where I talked too quietly, so I would like to do those louder. But I would love to record "I Slap Four" over, just because it was so much fun!

WILL

If you could be on any TV series of the last 25 years, which would it be and what kind of part would you play?

Katie

"Pee-Wee's Playhouse" had a super-fun set and cast. I think I would play a dentist. "The Office" would be fun too, and I could play a temporary office worker. My cartoon answer would be "Power Puff Girls" and "Pinky and the Brain." Those are my favorite cartoons I wasn't in.

WILL

Twenty questions down. When will Connie get a pet?

Katie

I thought she had one.

WILL

Are you a cat person or a dog person or another kind of person?

Katie

I really like Russian dwarf hamsters.

WILL

Will you ever tour the United States with an AIO show?

Katie

Yes! We are actually doing one now called "Fort Blanket Revue" with Phil Lollar! Funny you should ask this question, because you're in the same show. Good plug!

WILL

Why don't you write or direct an episode?

Katie

I have ideas for shows, but I'm not really a writer. I am amazed at how the writers do it. However, directing I would love to do, especially an episode with kids in it. I've asked several times if I could direct, and so far the answer seems to be "no" since I haven't done it. You should ask someone in charge about this.

More characters who have yet to appear in an Odyssey script:
(drawn by Will Ryan) "Lucky" O'Brien, proprietor of Lucky's Spitoon Empori-
um; Selma "Samba" LaZanga, dance instructor; Hucklebee Braindrizzle, town
chocoholic; Clatch Fimmery, visitor from out-of-town, occupation unknown.

WILL

Who is your favorite Darren on "Bewitched"?

Katie

The first one.

WILL

Does Connie Kendall carry a kindle?

Katie

She wants one . . . but she's leaning more towards an iPad with a Kindle app these days.

WILL

What are some of your favorite books?

Katie

"Peter Pan," "Heidi," and "Hind's Feet in High Places." And, of course, any book that you have ever written, including "The Tiny Little Book of Cowboy Haiku." Oh, and *this* one!

WILL

Do you think Officer David Harley will ever return to Odyssey?

Katie

Probably, but incognito.

WILL

Who is your favorite character that you've played on AIO, other than Connie?

Katie

Probably . . . Malanga! Because no one knew it was me.

WILL

What do you think about the various artistic representations of the Odyssey characters?

Katie

Seriously? Green leggings? Don't ask.

WILL

Thirty questions down—we're learnin' a lot! If Connie could go on some adventure to a foreign land, where would you like her to go?

Katie

Anywhere, but maybe Israel or Greece. I've been to Greece, but Connie hasn't. Neither of us has been to Israel.

WILL

Who are some of your favorite actors in movies and television?

Katie

Dennis Quaid, George Clooney, Cary Grant, Burt Reynolds, Cher, Meryl Streep . . . blah blah blah. I love good actors. They inspire me . . . to stay a voice actor. No, just kidding! I love watching their natural performances.

WILL

Have you ever ridden an elephant?

Katie

Yes, I think so. At a circus, but not "in" the circus.

WILL

Which episode of AIO means the most to you?

Katie

The very first one, because I thought it wasn't going to happen and then it did. And that's the one that started this whole wonderful odyssey. No pun intended.

WILL

After you've finished recording an episode, do you get to keep the clothes you wore during the taping?

Katie

"LOL!" I tried to keep yours, but you wouldn't let me.

WILL

How many times have you been to Whit's End at Focus on the Family's headquarters in Colorado Springs and do you have to pay for food there?

Katie

These questions are why I love you so much!! I have been to Whit's End at least seven times, I bet. Remember that first time we went there and they had this Grand Opening? No one invited us, but I wanted to go. I convinced you to go with me. Then I told Paul and he got worried. He thought if I went unsupervised and people recognized my voice that there would be chaos. So he decided to fly us out so they could keep an eye on us and manage us. So we ended up getting to go after all and we signed autographs. Do you remember? Do you?

And no, they usually feed us when we're on official business. I love that part!! I have been there on my own with my family too, but still usually manage a free treat at the Whit's End soda fountain. I like to go behind the counter and make stuff for the customers and pretend I'm Connie.

WILL

Do you prefer single episodes or two-parters or three-parters or twelve-parters or what?

Katie

I think single or three. After that I really don't know what's going on anymore. How about you?

WILL

What characters would you like to have return to Odyssey?

Katie

Rodney Rathbone!

WILL

What are your plans for the future?

Katie

To go to the next chapter. I'm tired of being interrogated like this! I wanna have a conversation!

4

Atque Vale!

In which, pursued by no ursine creatures,
our players gracefully exit

Katie

Do I go first again?

WILL

No. This time I go first.

Katie

Really?

WILL

Well, that was the plan, but it looks like you went first.

Katie

Oh good! So how did we do?

WILL

I'm not sure. I thought you would be the one to ramble on and on, but you actually gave a lot of really short answers—

Katie

Yeah, I guess I was thinking of lunch!

WILL

 —whereas surprisingly, in many of my responses I found myself eschewing terseness in favour of specificity and elucidation.

Katie

Yeah, you were ramblin' on, all right!

WILL

I feel I gave you an unfair amount of pages to blather. So go on.

Katie

What?

WILL

Please blather.

Katie

What do you mean "please blather"?

WILL

You know, yak away—the way you always do. We're very patient here.

Katie

"Yak away?" What are you talking about? "Yak away the way I always do"?! What does that mean! When I talk, I *say* something! I don't just throw out meaningless dribble—like an alphabetized list of names for planets—

WILL

Hey! I gave that list a lot of thought! They may need those when they colonize the moon! It was a public service!

Will the real CONNIE KENDALL PLEASE stand up!

G

H

I

J

K

L

Can you guess the identities of these Connie Kendall look-alikes?
(Answers on last page)

Katie

"Possible names for elves?" Is that a public service?! When I blather, which I hardly ever do, it's about important things!

WILL

Oh, "important things"! Like Russian dwarf hamsters?

Katie

Hey! That's important!

WILL

. . . Or your hitherto-unrevealed secret crush on film actor Dennis Quaid?

Katie

Hey! That's impor– Never mind!

WILL

. . . Or your complete ignorance as to Connie's middle name?

Katie

What?!

WILL

It's outrageous! Constance Kendall, an eighteen-year old student you've been essaying on the wireless for three decades – and you don't even have the common decency to remember her middle name!

Katie

Hey! I didn't say I forgot her middle name! I said *she* did!

WILL

Isn't that wonderful, I inquired sarcastically! Now you're attempting to pin the blame on a poor defenseless teenager who's not even here to speak up for herself! Mizz Kendall, I am—I mean: Mizz Leigh, I am shocked—shocked—shocked by your pusillanimous cravenness and near-sociopathic indifference towards fictional humanity!

Katie

What? Hey listen Mr. Ryan—I mean Professor Ryan, let me tell *you* a thing or two!

WILL

To paraphrase Sammy Shooster: if you can count that high, pray proceed.

Katie

First of all, I never blather. Sure, I can go on and on—and sometimes even on and on and on and on—about certain topics, but that's only because I'm enthusiastic and I enjoy sharing!

WILL

"Sharing"?

Katie
Yes, "Sharing"! A concept obviously foreign to you, which is why you order food no one else wants to eat!

WILL
I'm sharing this book with you!

Katie
True, but if I didn't start off each chapter on my own—*you* would have barged in ahead of me and I might not have been able to say a thing!

WILL
What?!

Katie
I'm not some big know-it-all who keeps a diary of all the fun he's having and uses big words to disguise the fact that he has absolutely nothing to say!

WILL
"Nothing to say"?! I selflessly provide the space program with a list of future geographic demarcations and you dare to accuse me of having nothing to say?!

Katie
Get serious!

WILL

I *am* serious! If I had nothing to say, you'd be writing this book all by yourself! And then where would you be?

Katie

I'd be a lot better off, I can tell you that! I'd be twice as better off! I'd make twice as much sense and I'd probably be twice as far along in writing this book too!

WILL

What?!

Katie

Yeah! Why, if I were writing this book by myself, I'd probably be all the way up to writing the—the—what do they call it?

WILL

The title?

Katie

No! The other thing.

WILL

The book proposal?

Katie

No, no! The watchama-callit!

WILL
The outline?

Katie
No! You know – the thing that comes after the first book!

WILL
The sequel?

Katie
Yeah, that's it! If I were writing this book all by myself, by now I'd probably be writing the sequel!

WILL
"The Care and Feeding of Russian Dwarf Hampsters: Part Two"?

Katie
Good idea! But let me tell you another thing!

WILL
Better hurry. We're running out of pages.

Katie
We are?

WILL
Indeed. Your tirade nearly rambled and blathered us right up to the finish line.

Katie

Oh no! There's a whole lot more I wanted to say!

WILL

Likewise. However I must admit to a certain amount of elation in regards to what I believe we have accomplished, working thusly in twain.

Katie

And what would that be?

WILL

Oh, you know.

Katie

You mean: We gave a small peak behind the scenes of two of the personalities who make up the longest-running professional dramatic series in the history of American radio?

WILL

Actually, I was thinking of something else we managed to accomplish herein—something far more important.

Katie

Well? What is it?

WILL

We have disproven, once and for all, the bizarre and ancient theorem that the personalities of Katie Leigh and Will Ryan are similar in any way, shape or form to those of Constance Kendall and Eugene Meltsner.

Katie

(pause)
What?! Are you crazy?!

WILL

I'll take that as a rhetorical question, but in case you're serious: No, I am not! That ridiculous afore-mentioned contention has now been disproven once and forever. Its antithesis is axiomatic.

(*Note to reader:* The following two speeches overlap each other.)

Katie

I have no idea what you're talking about and furthermore I don't care what you're talking about! If it were up to me, I'd never have to listen to another word that sprang out of that self-satisfied, so-called brain of yours! And I'd like to know who made YOU the King of This Book? And why I can't even mention that time you dreamed I was a giant chicken and I was buying you an upside-down pizza pie for Lincoln's birthday! And who put you in charge

Our two collaborators are seen here, reading about Elmo Aardvark®
en route to Colorado Springs for the opening hit's End, 1986. A
friendly flight attendant took this snapshot of Katie and Will, once
again posing in contemplative thought.

of telling me where to stop and start and accusing me of rambling on and on and on and on and—!

WILL

Of course you have no idea what I'm talking about. You generally have no idea what *you're* talking about! And neither does anybody else! If I had to listen to any more of you're ill-conceived, half-baked nonsense that you call "sharing," I'd rather be stranded on Monkey Island where discourse would be more comprehensible! And likely more enlightening! Why, if I didn't value this ukulele so much I'd be tempted to test its integrity by way of application to a certain unnamed noggin located in the general vicinity of second person singular. And another thing—!

(FADE OUT, AND . . .)

𝕿𝖍𝖊 𝕰𝖓𝖉.

(But wait . . . there's more . . .)

BONUS

CHAPTER

Aloha!

Wherein our interlocuters return many moons later; purportedly older and possibly wiser

FYTTE the FIRST

In which our heroes regroup

Katie

My turn?

WILL

No, I'm supposed to go first this time. We agreed on that last week after arguing about it for three years. Remember?

Katie

Oh. Right. Then go ahead.

WILL

Okay. I –

Katie

After I introduce you.

WILL

"Introduce" me?

Katie

Sure. Everybody needs an introduction.

WILL
Katie!

Katie
What?

WILL
Presumably they just read this whole book up to this point. They know who we are by now!

Katie
As I was saying: Everybody needs an introduction—especially the kind of person "who needs no introduction"!

WILL
Well, I can't argue with that....

Katie
Thanks.

WILL
…for the simple reason that I have no idea what it means.

Katie
Thank you again.
Ahem.
And now, ladies and gentleman, here to explain what this Epilogue is all about is someone who needs no introduction—

WILL

—hence this introduction—

Katie

—and who will explain to all of you that we've decided to add a Bonus Chapter to this new edition of "Adventures in Oddity" now that the 30th Anniversary of the radio series "***ADVENTURES IN ODYSSEY***" has come and gone.

WILL

Okay . . .

Katie

And to tell you how grateful we are to the many nice people who ordered the super-rare Limited Edition signed and numbered copies of our book in advance—way back in 2015 when it was first published.

WILL

True, but -

Katie

And to the even many-er other people who bought "Adventures in Oddity" in its rare, now out-of-print first edition!

WILL

Okay. So—

Still more characters who have yet to appear in an Odyssey script:
(Clockwise) Lonesome Hank Gregarious, proprietor Lucky Albatross Inn. Lysterine Johnson-Johnson, inventor of edible thumbtack. Ambiguo Epicene, about whom little is known. Furley Figüten, the man with more maps of Connelsville than any other human being in all of greater Connelsville. (drawn by Will Ryan)

Katie

And to also thank everybody who bought the hilarious Audio Book CD version, released way back in 2016 and still available, which features special guest appearances by famed writer, director and producer Phil Lollar and multi-talented rock star-turned-actor Ian Whitcomb.

WILL

Fine. Now –

Katie

Not to mention the added bonus on the Audio Book of our catchy performance of the hit song "All Aboard for Iggledip" which I personally play for my goldfish every day.

WILL

Really?

Katie

Don't interrupt. I'm introducing you.
He will also regale you with stories of how we've been besieged by people with more questions they wanted answered in "Adventures in Oddity".

WILL

Yes, and so –

Katie

Questions about our thoughts and feelings regarding our work on "***ADVENTURES IN ODYSSEY***," and other important topics like: Why did Will do all of the artwork and not let Katie do any?

WILL

Huh?

Katie

And: How come in that first edition, Will got to use all the big words?

WILL

What?!

Katie

Well, it's true. I think that hogging all of the very large big words was not nice 'cause it made you look smart and it made me look like a . . . like a . . .

WILL

"Like a Leika"? As in "I Am a Camera"?

Katie

No! It made me look like a . . . like a "nunce"!

WILL

"Nunce"?

Katie
"Nunce". It's Welsh. I looked it up. It means whatever I want it to.

WILL
All of my words mean what I want them to.

Katie
Really?

WILL
Zeally.

Katie
"Zeally"?

WILL
Zeally.

Katie
Wow.

WILL
There's fluppancy for you.

Katie
"Fluppancy"? What does "fluppancy" mean?

WILL

By "fluppancy" I mean that we've had quite enough of that topic, and it's high time we moved on to the next, which in this instance would be: explaining our plan for this all-new Bonus Chapter—

Katie

Which is . . . ?

WILL

—which is to make actual references to, and reveal actual thoughts from our actual beclouded recollections regarding the actual radio program we both actually work on.

Katie

It's about time.

WILL

It's about "*ADVENTURES IN ODYSSEY*" . . . actually.

Katie

And how are we going to do that?

WILL

By using a "proven successful" format.

Katie Which is?

WILL

—which is our *original* format from the first edition of "Adventures in Oddity," i.e., an opus of four distinct sections—

Katie

Which are . . . ?

WILL

—which are: Introductory remarks, followed by two sections wherein each of us peppers questions at the other, followed by closing remarks.

Katie

That's an awful lot for one word to mean; even if the word is, um . . . fluppancy?

WILL

Fluppancy.
Spelled the usual way.

Katie

Oh.

WILL

When I make a word do a lot of work like that, I always pay it extra.

Katie

Huh?

WILL
(wagging head gravely, from side to side)
Ah, you should see 'em come round me of a Saturday night.

Katie
What!?

WILL
For to get their wages, you know.

Katie
Oh. How do you pay 'em?

WILL
By the word, of course!

Katie
Of course. (beat) What?!

WILL
Inzactability!

Katie
What do you mean by "Inzactability"?

WILL
By "inzactability" I mean it's time for me to stop quoting Humpty

Dumpty, so that we can all proceed to the second section—or "fytte" as I prefer to term it—of this all-new Bonus Chapter.

Katie
Already?

WILL
Already.

Katie
But I'm not done introducing you yet!

WILL
Too late.

FYTTE the SECOND

Wherein Will pitches and Katie swings

Katie

Just to make things easier for you, I've made up a bunch of questions you can ask me.

WILL

What? That's not how this is supposed to work!

Katie

We did it your way before, and now we're doing it my way. Okay?

WILL

Well, okay. What's the first question I'm asking you?

Katie

What makes me so wonderful?

WILL

All right. What makes you so – WHAT??

Katie

Just kidding. Here's a big list.

WILL

It's a big list, all right.

Katie

A lot of people helped me with the questions. Pick any of them and fire away.

WILL

All right. Here's one: Who is the most Spirit-led person you've ever met?

Katie

Good question.

WILL

It's your own question.

Katie

I know. Good choice.

WILL

Thanks. I think.

Katie

On the show, I would say the most Godly character Connie ever met would be Malachi. Remember the angel?

WILL

Phillip Glassboro was terrific as Malachi!

Katie

I loved the way he came to help in that episode and how cool he was. However, in real life, if I wanted some good sound spiritual advice, I have a friend who works at Focus on the Family who is a wonderful counselor. I won't say her name because people would go looking for her. I often ask Chris Anthony Lansdowne her thoughts on spiritual matters, too. Outside of my AIO friends, there are many people I've met who operate in the spirit and inspired me to do the same. But when I was working on the Muppet Babies cartoon, I needed help with my singing. My director knew I was a Christian and sent me to a Christian singing teacher. She was a hoot and an inspiration at the same time. She would use bible verses to instruct in the singing lessons--probably out of context. For instance, to remind me to stand up straight, she would quote Jesus when He said, "If I be lifted up, I will draw all men unto me!" She would also share her wisdom with me with regard to my personal life. Her name was Laura Hart.

WILL

She sounds like a wonderful person. Here's another question: What's your favorite Bible episode on an Odyssey episode in which you "appeared"?

Katie

You know I loved "Back to Bethlehem" because it felt so real to me.

I felt like I was there at the birth of Jesus. The dialogue was quite clever. I actually just listened to it again at Christmas and enjoyed it all over again. I also like the BTV episodes, especially the one where we were all parts of the body, "BTV: Behind the Scenes"

WILL

Hooray for BTV! As Milton Berle used to remind me over lunch at the Friar's Club, "Funny is funny!" And as I'm reminding you now "Wacky is wacky!" I might also mention, by the by, that "Zany is zany, nutty is nutty, and cuckoo is koo-koo" but I'm not sure how much wisdom you're ready to absorb at this time. All right, back to my assigned task: "Most inspirational Odyssey episode?"

Katie

I loved the Underground Railroad and the Jubilee singers. I really enjoy listening to the historical, true stories we make shows about – even though I'm not in a lot of them. The story of Horatio Spafford who wrote the hymn "It Is Well With My Soul" really touched me. To lose his whole family like he did and still write praise songs to the Lord takes an amazing relationship with God. What an inspiration! He was sort of like a modern day Job—who could also write songs! Well, maybe Job could write songs, but I don't think it's mentioned anywhere in the Bible.

WILL

Maybe it's mentioned in that Qumran scroll I gave you for your birthday.

Katie

The what?

WILL

Oops. Must've been someone else. But you're right: Job might well have been an amazing blues singer. Quickly moving along: "Favorite people in the Bible episodes?"

Katie

Do you mean favorite people in the Bible who were portrayed in episodes? Or do you mean favorite people (i.e., actors) who played people in the Bible episodes?

WILL

I don't know what I mean. It's YOUR question!

Katie

Then I think I'll go with the first definition.

WILL

Please do.

Katie

Thank you.

WILL

I'm welcome.

Katie

Like Connie, one of my favorite people in the Bible is Ruth. She was such a good and faithful person to God and to her mother-in-law, and God took care of her. Her story was really romantic too. I have to say that Esther, is also one of my favorites. Not only was she brave, and saved her whole nation, but listening to Dave Madden as Bernard tell stories is always a treat. Besides that, my mother's name was Esther. You may remember that Earl Boen played King Xerxes who was a good guy, but he also played Dr. Blackgaard who, of course, was a bad guy.

WILL

Earl Boen is such a talented actor that he's actually oxymoronic.

Katie

Huh?

WILL

He's a very good bad guy! Okay, here's another question for you by you, which is apparently two questions: Do you remember the first Imagination Station visit to Biblical times? And what did you think of that?

Katie

I think the Imagination Station is an awesome way to experience the Bible. I believe the first such episode was the story of David and Goliath. Our engineers do such a wonderful job creating the ambience and sound effects that they draw you into the story right away. As you know, the episodes aren't so much Bible stories as

Bible *experiences* brought to life in such a way that kids and adults can get a glimpse into not only what life was like back then, but also what kinds of thoughts and feelings the characters might have had. The writing we have on Odyssey is very relatable.

WILL
I won't refer at this juncture to the talking chicken episode

Katie
Thanks. When I first did an Imagination Station script, I thought it was cool. But when I first HEARD an Imagination Station episode it was so exciting it just blew me away!

WILL
And that was before Start Trek came up with the holodeck!

Katie
It was?

WILL
If it wasn't, we'll certainly hear about it.

Katie
That's for sure.

WILL
Next from your list: Which episode would you like to go back to? (Syntax your own.)

Will the real
HARLOW DOYLE
PLEASE stand up!

M

N

O

P

Q

R

Can you guess the identities of these Harlow Doyle look-alikes?
(Answers on last pages)

Katie

If I could go back and re-record an episode, I think I would pick "Connie Comes to Town." It was my first episode, and it would be fun to start all over again. And of course, you weren't there yet.

WILL

Yeah, I—WHAT?

Katie

Just sayin'.

WILL

Katie—I was TOO there yet! It's just that *Eugene* wasn't there yet! But *I* was there, just as sure as my name is Officer Harley. Or Guy. Or—

Katie

Oh. Then never mind.

WILL

Say, if you went back and did that first Connie episode all over again, what if you gave her a French accent? Never mind, I forgot: You're asking my questions here. So here's another one: Do you think Connie's personality has changed as a result of her growing relationship with God?

Katie

I think she is still impulsive and sort of wears her heart on her sleeve. However, I do think she's much more aware of the presence of God, and the mystery of God, and the value of praying and reaching out to God on a regular basis. I know that for myself, as I see how God has worked in my life and in the lives of those around me, there is much more that I don't know than I do know. What I mean is: like Connie, I don't think I know as much now as I thought I knew when I was younger. So knowing that, I am a bit more hesitant as I get older to jump to conclusions.

WILL
I think I know what you mean.

Katie
Thanks.

WILL
In short, I think I know less than I thought I once knew when I thought I knew more than I think I do now. I think.

Katie
Is that what I said?

WILL
Who knows? (But remind me to set that whole thing to music.) Here's another: "Has anyone you know been influenced by AIO in a good way?" Hey! I already know the answer to this—and I happen to know that you've been working on a certain project relating to this question. But answer away!

Katie

So many fans have written letters that I've seen and therefore probably many more that I haven't, who have shared how various Odyssey episodes led them to accept Jesus as their Lord or helped them to work through decisions with which they were wrestling. Some of the best stories I hear are how people grew up listening to Odyssey, and sort of forgot about it until they became adults or were in college when they were confronted with some situation and an episode came to mind that helped them or guided them through it. There is one girl I met personally who said she was a sort of wild child. Her parents made her listen to Odyssey to try to steer her in the right direction. And it had the desired result. In fact, after that when she needed to be disciplined, they would take away her Odyssey listening privileges! Now she is actually an accomplished scriptwriter for faith-based radio theater!

WILL

While I'm being inquisitive, I'm gonna sneak in an "unofficial" question of my own now: You're actually putting together a whole book of such stories, right?

Katie

Yep. Well, not a *whole* book, but a book with lots of stories in it, as well as my OWN story!

WILL

Sounds sordid.

Katie

Yes, we're sorting out the stories right now.

WILL

But let's not spill any more beans about your upcoming tell-all, and move on to "Fytte the Third!"

Katie

I beg your pardon?

WILL

The next section of this chapter.

Katie

Oh. Okay!

FYTTE the THIRD

Wherein Katie poses and Will elucidates

Katie

Now it's my turn to come up with questions!

WILL

You came up with all the questions in the *previous* fytte!

Katie

Don't have a fit. I may have supplied them, but you got to ask them. Right?

WILL

I suppose so.

Katie

See? Fair is fair, right?

WILL

That would be axiomatic.

Katie

Okay, fair is axiomatic. But now it's my turn. So . . . Had you ever

worked on any faith based shows before "***ADVENTURES IN ODYS-
SEY?***" If so, how were they alike and how were they different?

WILL

It's been widely reported—and others seem to have clear recollections—that I worked on the predecessor of "***ADVENTURES IN
ODYSSEY,***" viz. "Family Portrait." People also have told me that
I was on a Salvation Army-produced radio series. The difference
between those series and the current one is that I distinctly remember my initial and ongoing involvement in the present series. My
involvement in the earlier two series does however seem entirely
possible.

Katie

Can I interrupt your answer?

WILL

No.

Katie

That would be "Heartbeat Theater" with the Salvation Army, I bet!
I used to sneak in to watch those recordings. Bob Luttrell was the
engineer on those sessions, and he was also our first engineer on
Adventures in Odyssey. He probably recommended you for AIO.
Hal Smith, Walker Edmiston, and Parley Baer also worked on
Heartbeat Theater.

WILL

—and a lot of well-known movie stars, too.

Katie

Bob didn't recommend *me* for "Odyssey" though, because I never actually worked on any of the shows. I just used to hang out during them. He thought I was just a pest. He didn't know I could act.

WILL

I said "No" to interrupting. Evidently I meant "be my guest".

Katie

Evidently. Thank you.

WILL

Think nothing of it.

Katie

Okay.

WILL

And if Bob ever actually did think of you as a "pest," it was probably as a very nice, attractive, clean and fun-loving pest.

Katie

(flattered) Thanks! Wow, you really think I'm clean?

WILL

You almost always throw your trash away at the end of recording sessions. I notice little things like that.

Characters whose voices were never heard in an Odyssey episode:
(Clockwise) Merrivale T. Mildew, guppie impersonator; Blaise Blasé, silent auctioneer and official Will Ryan Radiogenic Cap model; Bunkarino Pizzacato, founding member of the Bavarian All-Saw Orchestra; Madame Güseflesche, subatomic contralto. She sings in registers only dachshunds can hear.

Katie

I do, don't I?

WILL

"Next to Godliness", that's Katie! To continue: After Odyssey was established, I distinctly remember working with Earl Boen, and possibly with Walker Edmiston too, on a few episodes of another faith-based series sometime in the 1990s. The tone of those particular episodes was rather dark, as I recall. Since I generally prefer carrots to sticks, and milk and honey to fire and brimstone, I found "*ADVENTURES IN ODYSSEY*" more enjoyable a series than whatever that other one was. I never received a copy of—or heard—the finished product, although I know it was released and/or broadcast.

Katie

Sounds mysterious.

WILL

"Jungle Jam" is a great audio series, co-created by Phil Lollar. One fine day, the Saguaro Sisters and I were talking with Phil about Jungle Jam, and I said I really wish that I had worked on that wonderfully entertaining, song-filled show. Then Phil suddenly remembered that you and I had each made a guest appearance on that series! …the girls confirmed it and then…I remembered it, too! … My wish came true—in retrospective advance, I think! Do YOU remember being a guest on "Jungle Jam", oh Katie Leigh?

Katie

Now that I'm reminded of it . . . yes, I think I do. I also remember wishing I had a bigger part.

WILL

I think door slams were involved in our appearances. By the way, there is an old axiom— known to actors throughout the world – which I have just made up: "There are no small parts, only small paychecks."

Katie.

Oh. Well, next question: You have portrayed many different Bible story characters on the show. Which ones stand out to you the most?

WILL

According to Nathan Hoobler –

Katie

writer, director and mental archivist? THAT Nathan Hoobler?

WILL

The same. According to Nathan Hoobler, who seems to possess a breezy omniscience regarding all things "*ADVENTURES IN ODYSSEY*," I have thus far performed well over 100 characters on the series. That accounting might help explain why it's a little hard for me to answer your question. But, undaunted, I persevere. Answer: I'm still amazed that I was the voice of a well-known Son of a certain woman named Mary in at least one episode. Over a thirty-some-year period, there have probably only been six or seven of us who played that role on the series. Actually, Nathan could tell us.

But in contrast, there was another episode wherein Ian Whitcomb played, I think, Pontius Pilate and I played another antagonist of the aforementioned estimable Paraclete. That seemed odd, because both Ian and I are such nice guys in real life. And we're both ukulele players of some repute, too. (Ian wrote the delightful book "Ukulele Heroes", which I highly recommend.)

I think the one Biblical character Eugene should meet up with—and hang around with—is Solomon. And I suppose by that I mean that *I* would like to meet up with and hang around with Solomon. First of all, Solomon was said to be pretty wise; well, the wisest man in the world, anyway. Eugene would, generally speaking, appreciate the opportunity of "hobnobbing with his fellow wizard". Also, Solomon wrote a lot of songs—over 1,000 reportedly. Which brings to mind Steve Allen, who was also a pretty smart fellow and who happened to write more than 7,000 songs! Although I haven't met King Solomon yet, I was lucky enough to have known Steve Allen and his zesty wife "Janie Bird". Steve was a literate and funny television host for many decades, a prodigious author, a swell jazz pianist, a quick wit, and a responsible television producer. He created the television (and later radio) series "Meeting of the Minds", which was pretty much Steve's version of an Imagination Station panel talk show. The "guests" were great figures from world history. Steverino, as creator and writer of the series, properly cast himself as its host and moderator (I suppose that's one way to balance having done a series wherein your writers had you do things like jumping into a vat of Jello and acting with the Marquis Chimps). Steve had a strong impact on American popular culture throughout his years of television duties. It was on his program that a young Elvis

Presley introduced the song "Hound Dog," a foundational Rock 'n' Roll recording. Steve once devoted an entire hour to an up-and-coming songwriting folk-singer named Bob Dylan. Steve was very much responsible for the fame of such comedians as Don Knotts, Tom Poston, Louie Nye, Pat Harrington, Bill "Jose Jimenez" Dana and others. But I realize as I list these names, these talented folks may not have endured as stellar personalities in the public's memory as long as I would have liked (I mention this because I have met recent graduates of American universities who are unfamiliar with such giants of Show Biz as Laurel & Hardy, Bob Hope and Johnny Carson. *Sic transit gloria mundi*.) Steve Allen also promoted jazz artists and singers. And great books. Among Steve's last campaigns as a concerned citizen was trying to solve the problem of the American media's abandonment of ethical responsibility. I wish he had lived longer. It seemed—and seems—a nearly unsolvable problem and I'd love to see what he might have come up with.

Katie

I saw you play music at the Steve Allen Theater!

WILL

That's right! Will Ryan & the Cactus County Cowboys performed "The Will Ryan Cactus County Round Up" with tons of special guests for an entire year at the Steve Allen Theater in Hollywood.

Katie

That show was so much fun! And the band is TERRIFIC!

WILL

An uncontestable declaration! By the way, Steve Allen began his career in Los Angeles radio in post-war 1940s as the star and host of the "Smile a While" morning show. Our pal June Foray, the Hollywood Voice Legend who is heard on one of the Odyssey videos, by the way, was a regular on every episode as his girlfriend Janie.

Speaking as we are of great figures from world history, Solomon is the only Biblical character whose initial is used to form the letters in the name of the ancient wizard "Shazam" (the wisdom of Solomon, the strength of Hercules, the stamina of Atlas, etc.). Shazam, of course, is the name that the boy reporter Billy Batson must cry out to be changed—by a bolt of lightning—into Captain Marvel, World's Mightiest Mortal. Quite a rare distinction, I'd say. I'd like to ask Solomon what he thinks of that!

I really enjoyed the episode with Shadrach, Meshach and Abednego. You don't get to pronounce those three names together too often, but we sure did on THAT episode! Law firm, anybody?

Katie

They sure were strong in their faith, weren't they?

WILL

They certainly were. I'm sure they couldn't stand Nebuchadnezzar – but who could? I think the plot of the third "Toy Story" film may have benefitted from their experience, by the way. But speaking of Shadrach, Meshach and Abednego (and not to mention Nebuchadnezzar), I think we should do a special "*ADVENTURES IN ODYSSEY*" episode wherein we meet all the characters in the Bible who possess difficult-to-pronounce names. Phil Lollar, Dave Arnold and Nathan Hoobler could consult with Biblical and linguistic scholars aforehand, achieve definitive pronunciational consensus, and then we could record this special episode clearly and distinctly. And thus we could benefit mankind and posterity!

Katie
Uh . . . sure. Okay.

WILL
I smell another Peabody Award.

Katie
"Another"?

WILL
Although I resolutely maintain I did not earn it, I do happen to be the proud owner of an actual Peabody Award, the most prestigious award given for quality broadcasting.

Katie
I never knew that!

WILL
I never talk about it. Please try to be more discreet next time.

Katie
I shall. Wait a minute!

WILL

Never mind. Let's go back to your question regarding Biblical characters. I wrote a song about Job once. He sure got a pretty raw deal there for a while. If we ever do go back in the Imagination Station and meet up with him, maybe we can sing him that song to cheer him up a bit. I wonder if he likes ukulele music.

Katie

Many blues singers do.

WILL

No foolin'?

Katie

I imagine.

WILL

Oh. And I'd really like to know more about a certain Rabmag known as Nergalsharezar, who is mentioned in Jeremiah as a prince of Babylon. I hope Eugene and Connie bump into him via the Imagination Station too, so we can find out more!

Should Sampson sound like Victor Mature? I hope so.

And speaking on non sequiturs, Hopalong Cassidy – in the person of actor William Boyd—appears as Simon of Cyrene with Jesus in the early Cecil B. DeMille epic, 1927's "The King of Kings". June Foray worked not only with us – but with Hoppy too, on a recording for Capitol Records! Which was also Tennessee Ernie's long-time label! And, of course, the Beatles! And June and I met Paul McCartney at the Oscars once – we were kind of stuck on an Otis elevator with him! And Otis is the character Hal Smith played on "**THE ANDY GRIFFITH SHOW**"! And Otis spelled backwards is Sito! And Tom Sito – or was it Eric Goldberg?— is the guy who INTRODUCED us! It's ALL so amazingly INTERTWINED!!

Katie

The mind boggles. Ahem. Continuing: Have you ever been to the Holy Land?

WILL

No. I prefer the Imagination Station. Generally speaking, I feel more at ease in environments where uniformed, machine gun-toting teenagers are not patrolling the streets.

Katie

You're not as adventurous as I thought you were.

WILL

I know. Many a mook has been misled by a solar topi. (That's one of the many reasons I don and endorse that radiogenic wonder known as the Official Will Ryan Cap – handmade in the USA by Bree. Get one now!) "Caution is the wiser part of valor" say I. And, yes, you may quote me. But speaking of holy *land*, if there is still any sanctified soil left in that contested realm – meaning earth upon which Jesus might have actually trod—historians and geologists can argue as to how far below the present ground level it may be. Twenty feet? Forty? I've been to Stratford-upon-Avon where what is presented as the home of William Shakespeare likely has not a single wattle or daub—nor a sole whit or iota—of anything that may have been there in the days of the Bard. And of course that was a mere four hundred-some years ago. When I first set foot on the Disney lot in the 1970s, it was much the same as when Walt last saw it a decade earlier. The studio is very different today and will undoubtedly be even more different in another four or five decades.

The Holy Land is roughly the size of New Jersey and I haven't even seen all of *New Jersey* yet! I spent two summers working in Cape May, a delightful town filled with beautiful Victorian "gingerbread" structures. I stayed in Fort Lee, birthplace of the Movie Business and home to Thomas Edison's "Black Maria" film studio, wherein Annie Oakley, J. Stuart Blackton, Fred Ott, "Happy Hooligan" and many others were immortalized on film. I look forward to seeing more than a glimpse of the town of Patterson, famed as the birthplace of Bud Abbott's comedy partner Lou Costello. The foundations of each of these cities are *still* the same distance from the Earth's centre as they were when all of those notable events occurred. I find that relatable.

Katie
Well, speaking of relating to things: When Eugene was having his existential crisis, could you relate?

WILL
If I couldn't, the show might have been pretty bad. But, for a lot of reasons, it's great. I'm just glad I've never had to play Job.

Katie

Did you ever go to vacation Bible school when you were a kid? What about church camp?

WILL

Yes. It was a bit of both. And I can still remember the theme song we sang on the bus. I didn't realize it at the time, but it was set to the tune of something else. I'm humming it now to figure out what the original tune was. Ah yes! Although the syllabification was different enough from the original to obscure the source (and the time signature was changed from a jaunty 2/4 to a spirited march tempo), the basic tune was actually appropriated from the verse of "The Ballad of Davy Crockett". The Davy Crockett song was written for Walt Disney's filmed portrayal of the famed frontiersman, congressman, humourist, author and Western pioneer by two great musical talents. Film composer George Bruns wrote that tune to fit screenwriter Tom Blackburn's multitudinous lyrics. The composition, an early personal favourite, is impressive on a number of counts:

> ONE: It has a four-rhyme scheme for each verse. That's relatively rare.
> TWO: It has over 20 verses! That's pretty unusual these days.
> THREE: It has a very simple, singable and catchy chorus.
> FOUR: It was so popular a song, it took over the nation!
> FIVE: It has one of the longest titles of any song that ever made the Top Ten.

None of the other songs we sang at camp were as well-crafted, including the pastiche we sang on the bus. As a kid I wondered if George Bruns was related to George Burns, or if he was possibly a typographical error. I did grow up to meet the comedian George Burns; his office was directly below mine for a few years. It was on Seward Street and whenever I walked into the building and smelled his cigar smoke I knew all was well in Show Biz. I never did meet the skilled composer and orchestrator George Bruns when I was ensconced at Disney's, though I knew many people who knew him. I vaguely recall that one day I heard that he had been visiting Disney music publishing a week or so before I had asked about him (or maybe it was Disney composer Buddy Baker. Or, more likely, both.) That's as close as I got to the great composer of "Davy Crockett" and Walt Disney's "Zorro" television series.

Katie
I used to watch Zorro!

WILL
Well worth watching. Walt himself supervised the first 26 episodes. After that, "Walt Disney Productions" was in charge. The full title of the Davy Crockett song, as written on the cover of the first edition sheet music published by Wonderland Music Company, is:

The BALLAD of DAVY CROCKETT

HIS EARLY LIFE, HUNTING ADVENTURES, SERVICE UNDER GENERAL JACKSON IN THE CREEK WAR, ELECTIONEERING SPEECHES,

CAREER IN CONGRESS, TRIUMPHAL TOUR IN THE NORTHERN
STATES, AND SERVICES IN THE TEXAN WAR.

We had the Bill Hayes recording of that song in our house when I
was diminutive. That's the rendition that hit Number One on the
Hit Parade during the Davy Crockett craze. Two other recordings – by Fess Parker and Tennessee Ernie Ford—were also in the
Top Ten. That's way back in time when there actually was a Music
Business! As I write this, I just had dinner two days ago with two
people who had Bill Hayes as a guest on their popular Palm Springs
radio program last week. Fess Parker was a great hero of mine. I
was lucky to get to know him and spend many hours with him. I
could say a lot about him here, but I suspect I may be getting a tad
off track. (And speaking of getting off-track, although I never met
Tennessee Ernie Ford, I did work with some of his musicians and I
did sing on two albums for Disney's in a Nashville studio "the old
peapicker' frequented in his later years.)

Back on track: I only went to that aforementioned camp but once,
as my grandparents lived on a farm and we kids were needed to
help with agrarian duties every summer – and autumn and spring
(we got winters off, for the most part). I reckon summer camps –
Bible or otherwise—are more for city folks.

Katie
Well, how about something you DID do? When you worked for
Disney, what did you do THERE? And how was the food in the
commissary?

WILL

Two questions, yielding two answers. One: This and that. Two: Fine.

Katie

Do you have a favorite book of the Bible?

WILL

Is Genesis everyone's favourite book? There are a lot of reasons it might be. Or maybe Psalms? Or Proverbs? Or how about Matthew? He scoops everybody with his coverage of the Sermon on the Mount, so he wins a lot of points. "My favourite"? I shall have to ponder further.

Katie

Please do. I can wait.

WILL

I meant later. The answer may end up being a whole other book.

Katie

Keeping us in suspense, are you? Then I'll ask another question.

WILL

As is your wont.

One more character who has yet to appear in an Odyssey script:

Humidor "Flurg" Flurgison, Jr. III holds the distinction of having appeared in the least number of Adventures in Odyssey scripts, beginning with the very first script in which he was not credited due to his non-appearance. Although many other individuals may claim not to have appeared in an equal number of scripts, none have not done so with such conspicuous determination as Flurg.

Katie

I know you can read Latin, but can you also read Greek?

WILL

I'm afraid I'm like the Roman senator Casca in this regard. One fine day in ancient Rome – the Feast of the Lupercal in 44 BC at around a quarter past noon, if memory serves – Casca was questioned by Brutus about the content of Cicero's just-concluded oration. With his customary Shakespearean-penned dry wit Casca replied, "Those that understood him smiled at one another and shook their heads; but, for mine own part, it was Greek to me."

About the only Greek I recognize readily is the letter *pi*. And even then, I can only translate *pi* to about the fifth decimal point. But fear not, world; I have a computer in a secret location that's been working night and day on the problem of a complete translation of *pi* into its numerical equivalent. The computer has been on this task for seventeen years. It may conclude its job any moment now – or any year, or any century. Wish us luck!

And that's only one tiny *letter* of Greek which I can claim to partially comprehend! That particular language is a mountain I have thus far declined to ascend.

Those ancient Greeks! First they gave us the language, then they came up with the Labyrinth! They left us many wonderful things, but they also caused no little vexation. As the monkish scribes of olden times used to pen on their papyri, "*Graecum est; non legitur*".

That roughly translates to "Hey, pal – this part's written in Greek, so don't ask ME to figger it out!"

Katie

We know you play ukulele and guitar, but if you lived in Bible times, what instrument do you think you would have played?

WILL

If I painted you a picture of my answer, one of us might be a lyre.

Katie

Should we end this "fytte" on that terrible pun?

WILL

I prefer to think of it as a delightfully serendipitous verbal ambiguity, but to answer your question directly . . . Indubitably!

WILL

Well, we did it!

Katie

Did what?

WILL

We finished three grand fyttes, leaving but one to go!

FYTTE the FOURTH

Wherein, not unlike a toga, it's a wrap.

Katie
No, there's not.

WILL
What do you mean "No, there's not"?

Katie
There's *not* another "fytte". You talked so much that we ran out of space and we're done!

WILL
Really?

Katie
Zeally.

WILL
Zeally?

Katie
Really!

WILL
Zowie!

The End.

Portrait of the Authors, August 2020
or, "Will the real Connie and Eugene
please speak up."

Katie

Pssst! Hey, everybody!
This time *I* get the last word!

WILL

Congratulations, Katie!
I concede. *You* got the
final word!

Answers to
"Will the real Connie Kendall please stand up!"

Page 53:
(A) Taylor Swift, once-obscure singer; (B) Connie Stevens, movie star; (C) Daisy Mae Scaggs-Yokum, the Rose of Dogpatch; (D) Teresa Brewer, singer and 3D movie star; (E) Judy Jetson, teenager of the future; (F) Janet Waldo, eternal teenager and voice of Joanne on *Adventures in Odyssey*.

Page 80:
(G) Brigitte Bardot, gamin; (H) Pat Suzuki, "Miss Pony Tail"; (I) Pony Tail by Lee Holley; (J) Little Dot, as pictured by Steve Muffatti; (K) Ann-Margret, all-American Swedish sweetheart; (L) Tuesday Weld, who is cute any day of the week.

Answers to
"Will the real Eugene Meltsner please stand up!"

Page 20:
(A) D. David Eisenhower; (B) Beetle "Spider" Bailey; (C) Bill "Windows" Gates; (D) Peter "Herman" Noone; (E) Jimmy "Henry Aldrich" Lydon; (F) Barack Hussein Obama

Page 40:
(G) Sterling Holloway; (H) John "Beatles" Lennon; (I) Carl Barks' Gyro Gearloose; (J) George "Superman" Reeves; (K) Eugene Meltsner, as drawn by Will; (L) Daniel "Harry Potter" Radcliffe

Answers to
"Will the real Harlow Doyle please stand up!"

Page 110:
(M) Lester Gooch's Fearless Fosdick by Al Capp; (N) Basil
Rathbone as Sherlock Holmes; (O) Alex Raymond's Rip Kirby;
(P) Inspector John J. Fadoozle disguised as Howdy Doody; (Q)
Humphrey Bogart as Sam Spade; (R) Will Ryan's Ace Strongjaw
disguised as Harlow Doyle.

The ODDITY Appreciation Society

MEET THE FANS!

These are just a few unsolicited kudos from enterprising fans who were able to glom onto an early draft of this exciting *NEW Bonus Chapter Edition*. Naturally, they were immediately overcome with ziposity. Below are their laudatory exultations and their likenesses captured by our staff cartoonist, Prof. Zeus.
Random Sampling #7301

S.S. Shmifflebog

"Zappy! Despite my best efforts, none of the pages came loose in my book!"

"Dixie" Flupper

"Zoomy! The ink literally leaps off the page in a fandango of terpsichorean abandon!"

Chumlia Plep

"A sweet reet pleat. I weighed this book and found it more than sufficient. A must have!"

Alfia Q. Bluten

"A kleede read, indeed! The paper stock delights every sense, without hint of offense!"

Zoop Finster

"Rignificent! And dare I say devoid of any staples, either eensy or humungious"

Potatoe W. Jeeble, PhD.

"Zubilee to the Nth! Call me Bumble U. Fumbled, but this here is a book!"

*"Ne Jupiter
Quidem Omnibus
Placet."*

Will Ryan
can be booked for
voice work through the offices of

Arlene Thornton & Associates
Tel: (818) 760-6688
arlene@arlenethornton.com

·

Katie Leigh
can be booked for
voice work or vocal coaching
through her website,
www.katieleigh.com

·

Will Ryan, KatieLeigh, and Phil Lollar can be
booked for personal appearances through

CelebWorx
Celebrity Representation
(818) 621-9148.

email:
nerylemus.rep@gmail.com
chrisarsaga.celebworx@gmail.com

·

The Official Will Ryan Radiogenic Cap
by Bree is available for purchase through
www.katieleigh.com

·

"When in the Milky Way, visit Iggledip!"

Hey everybody! Don't
tell You-Know-Who,
but I got the last word!

—*Katie*